POWER OF A WOMAN

BY

ROBERT GRAHAM JR

When a man deems a woman to be sacred, he's not focused on what she has achieved, but what she will. He's not looking at where she is, but where she will be. The mystery of sacred is in becoming, not always in being.

Acknowledgement

Dedicated to Deidra Cade, ("Sacred") May the Almighty majestic and eternal Yahweh through the messiah Yashua be forever glorified in this timely masterpiece.

You are my editor, agent/power of attorney and accountability partner all-in-one.

This profound read unveils the power of a woman and the impact that has been made in my life. "Sacred", you're most magnificent, royal and pure. You're the provocation and incentive behind the fulfilling of my dreams. Without you, I could hardly be me for you've provided for me completion. Through you I've found purpose, stability, joy and peace. You challenge me, and propel me forward. Your willingness to take a chance on me has rebirthed my authorship, creativity, talents and visions. You are funny, loyal and full of love and philanthropy. I have to say you are truly a work of the Creator's hand in my life!

Let's keep achieving great things!

To Bishop T.D. Jakes,

Your ministries and existence in this life has had more effect on my life than any man, living or dead. Following your ministry from its conception in West Virginia was the most astounding and closest example of a man to me til' this day. When you moved to Texas, the most dynamic impact on my search for manhood ensued. However, it wasn't until you founded "The Potter's House" that I started spiraling out of control and into criminal behavior. I've followed you from the four walls and bars in the South Carolina Department of Correctional facility. You prophesied in the mid 90's that there was going to come some men out of prison that was going to surprise "everybody". The message you preached about the Kingdom going to the dogs was another message of inspiration for me. I've listened to easily hundreds of your messages, but these two caused me to search the scriptures to ascertain what kind of madness is the bishop preaching. That's when I discovered Isaiah 42: 5-9, Ecclesiastes 4: 9-12, Zechariah 9: 11-12 and Psalm 102: 11-18 which established the foundation. Fast forward 20 years later and it was revealed to me that there is a shifting in the realm of the spirit.

Get ready! Get ready Bishop! The time is near!

CHAPTER ONE

From behind prison walls serving a life sentence without the possibility of parole, I met her. Well, not in person but I was introduced to her being. I was an aspiring urban novel writer in need of an agent/editor and a trustworthy power of attorney. A publishing company wasn't going to touch my handwritten manuscripts. Almost 21 years into my sentence at the Perry Correctional Institute in Pelzer, South Carolina while participating in the character based program called CBU Q1. The opportunity was presented to me to sign up for this creative writing class taught by two women named Anna Catherine and Carolyn. In this class I became aware of prompts, how to write story lines, the importance of details, dialogue, background, etc. It was very informative and introduced an opportunity to succeed from behind prison walls as a known author.

After completing the class successfully and receiving my certificate, I became impressed with autobiographies and urban novels written by former inmates like Terry Woods, Vicky Stringer, Alfred "Sha born" Adams, Jr. and Wahida Clark. They have gone on in society to publish great works and some even started their own publishing outlets. Reading their works is what inspired me to pursue my dreams of becoming a published author. I wrote poetry, and books in different genres but I realized at some point my journey was going nowhere fast unless I could find an agent, editor and power of attorney that would act on my behalf to propel my mission forward. Since I had no one I could readily rely on and entrust with this venture, I began to brainstorm and start my own grassroots movement of networking from within the prison. I was desperate and hungry for success.

At least a year had passed without any potential candidates, but my ambition and determination to find an agent got greater day by day. I talked to hundreds of inmates about potential family members or friends out in society that could possibly lend a brother a helping hand. I even turned to churches. It was my goal to leave no stone unturned. I gave 100% effort but it felt like a steel wall stood in the way of my dream. People were consistently saying "No!", "No, I'm sorry. I don't know anyone" (even if they did). I also asked the teachers of the class to no avail. Not to mention, I was often met with contempt and disdain, along with a bunch of naysayers who couldn't believe in me because they didn't believe in themselves. In spite of this, there was a relentless fire burning down deep inside of me that wasn't bowing to this opposition. I felt like I was embarking on a mission that wasn't just about me. I knew numerous incarcerated men who wrote page-turners possibly greater than myself but had not the determination to network and promote their own authorship. I felt I had to be the example for them.

CHAPTER TWO

I kept my faith and kept looking because faith without actions is dead. I was waiting for Yahweh to open the door. In the mean time I was also writing more and more novels and envisioning my dream. I saw myself being the talk of social media and having my work advertised on the radio in South Carolina. I had everything to gain and nothing to lose. My goal was not only to succeed myself but to be a conduit for others to do the same.

Moving forward to how I met "her".

It was around July 2014, there was this guy who worked with me in the cafeteria. They called him "King". I was sitting during my break looking through the huge glass from inside the kitchen when I heard King talking to someone behind me. I turned to my right to look in his direction when something took hold inside of me. It was a spirit that prompted me to take action to ask him one more time. I had previously talked with him about my goal with no results. I had to be sure. As he turned towards me to greet me, respectfully as always, I knew I couldn't let the moment pass. I said, "Brother, I need to ask you just one more time are you certain that you don't know anyone who has the creativity, open mind and has their wits about themselves that could help me publish my books?"

For a moment, the dynamic in the kitchen shifted. He put his right hand up under his chin and thought deep with what seemed like a lifetime to me, but about 30 seconds in reality. Then he looked up into my desperate eyes and said, "Yeah...man, I believe I do!" I wanted to weep like a newborn baby in that instance but I kept my composure. He let me know that the person was not his family member. He said, "There is this sista I know by the name of Deidra. Her brother's name is "Junior" I've talked to her on the phone and she seems a lot like you, intelligent and smart. I believe she's the one. I just need to ask him and get him to ask her."

All the while I was waiting for this moment, my manuscripts had been floating around the institution so lots of people had heard about me and it was highly likely Junior did too. About a week later in the cafeteria while I was working, King walked up to me with a white piece of paper in his hand and a cheesy smile on his face. He extended his right hand towards me and said, "This is Deidra's address. She's waiting to hear from you. Her brother is coming to meet you tomorrow." My jaw dropped. King wasn't the type of dude to lie or play games so I had no reason to doubt him. I hugged him after politely taking the address out of his hand as I thought to myself, "has heaven moved for little ole me?"

The very next day, Junior shows up just as King said he would. This was my first time meeting and communicating with him. We sat at a table in the kitchen and talked. He gave me the rundown and absolute assurance about his sister, Deidra. He said, "She's my sister. She is not the one to play games, I promise. The both of you have a lot in common." I guess King told him about my way of life and knowledge of history especially when it comes to slavery's impact on the behavioral and economic conditions of Africans in America. Over time he and I got more acquainted.

A week passed without my writing Deidra. Somehow I had lost my drive, and ambition. I think the hindrance was based on my experience with past black women raised in the south. They didn't seem to have anything to offer a brother besides their body and a lot of drama. I wasn't about to get played by sending her my manuscripts for her to steal my storylines and/or keep my books. I had no way to secure my copyright or to prove the manuscripts were mine. This woman was also a complete stranger to me. In the back of my mind I wondered (for days) if I was I being set up.

Seeing Junior in the cafeteria again was the tipping point I needed. He said, "I talked to Deidra during visit (time allocated for prisoners to get to spend time with their loved ones). I told her about your books. She's waiting to hear from you."

 I looked him in his eyes and didn't discern any foul play. So, I rushed to the dorm, sat down. I wrote her an extended letter about myself, and my interest in her helping me/us to do something extraordinary. I was going for broke, "Maryland-style". She responded to my letter promptly.

It was the most profound and detailed letter I'd ever received since incarceration. She seemed shy and unsure of the direction she should take. As this was the first time she had ever attempted to do anything of this fashion as far as being a literary agent, editor, etc. Not exactly what I had in mind, however she seemed very intelligent, optimistic and ambitious as I was. My gut told me she was the one.

CHAPTER THREE

We had a lot in common, and agreed on almost everything, which was a game changer for me. She seemed very honest and open about her life, dreams and visions. We communicated through the prison phone or by mail. We made arrangements for my first two manuscripts to be mailed to her. They were "Pimpin' Preacher & The Ruthless Drug Dealer" and "The Illusional Illusive Peeping Tom". They were two short stories that were to be combined into one book. I also had the niece of a friend inside help with the typing and was initially brought on to be an investor to help get the books published. I handwrote contracts for all parties involved (bless her cause my handwriting was atrocious) and Deidra typed them up then distributed them for all parties to sign. She also made copies for everyone to have as well.

The show was officially on the road. During our correspondence about the project she brought ideas and asked for my thoughts. She seemed scary submissive and not as aggressive as the women from my past. She was professional and business minded even though this was all new to her. These characteristics were important to me because one of the contracts included her being my Power of Attorney (Yes! You read that right.). I needed someone to act on my behalf and in my best interest on the outside. The fact that you are given this type of position from anyone speaks volumes. I felt I could give her that authority and she would not abuse it.

She worked a full-time job and was raising a teenaged son, all while taking on this task. She always seemed to be trying to improve herself on a personal and business level even though she had a bachelor's degree in engineering from Clemson University. She read different books and attended webinars online that helped her take her growth to the next level. Although, I felt and still feels she has everything she needs to succeed already. After the books were typed, then began the process of editing and critiquing. She sent some parts back to me to rewrite as well.

As time went by, life happened. We both went through unforeseen circumstances but still had our eyes on the goal ahead. I was placed in solitary confinement for about 4 ½ months for striking an officer and possession of a cellphone. Trust me, it's not how it sounds. This was my first real incident in the history of my incarceration. It was a freak dilemma. I did the time for it, which gave me plenty of time to think. I was eventually allowed back into population, thankfully!

Deidra stuck by me the entire time. She encouraged and reminded me to stay focused on the goal even though my predicament was not ideal. She also had her own obstacles as well in dealing with the murder of Austin's father a month before his graduation. I know it had to be a hard time, but she still remained vigilant about what we were trying to do. There was beauty in her brokenness. She managed to find some joy in the midst of all her pain.

Even with her power of attorney status she didn't try to pull rank or check me. She would eventually be the one who had control over any royalty checks produced from sales of the book. She proved herself to be trustworthy and dependable.

As we communicated about the progress of the book, I also began to tell her more of my life story. I mean all of it; every detail that made me the person I am. She knew more about me than my mom or the two wives that I had in the past. I told her about my past womanizing and sexist ways and much more. She'd listen quietly then respond kindly and briefly. She was not judgmental nor a talkative person. This seemed to absolutely be a miracle to me. You don't encounter many people like that. As I was writing this book on this day of April 18, 2016, I still have not seen her in person. Almost two years has passed. She's taught me about the power of faith and trust in a woman.

She has my life in her hands and she knows it. She's a southern "country" woman that's sophisticated and sacred with a heart of gold.

CHAPTER FOUR

We encountered financial struggles as the initial investors that were supposed to help finance the publishing and advertising fell through when it was time to do so. It further delayed the process. So, I went on another networking spree soliciting family, friends, etc. who could also benefit from investing with this project as they would also receive a percentage. My brother, Ronnie eventually came on board to contribute $90.00 towards the marketing. In return I offered him 1% of sales. We drew up the contracts to reflect the deal. Deidra was able to negotiate with the initial intended investor, Donshae who couldn't afford to help at the time. She struck a deal that would reinvest her payment for typing the Peeping Tom manuscript into the budget for marketing, which would entitle Donshae to 1.5% of sales from the book instead of just the flat fee payment. However, it still was not enough to cover publishing and the remaining advertising costs. Also, Ronnie later changed his mind about wanting to invest in this journey, so his funds were returned.

Initially, my stance was to not have Deidra contribute one red cent towards this project. I was out to impress her and to prove to her that I was a mover and a shaker even from prison. I was determined to make things happen. However, during this time, my connections proved failing and unreliable. I hit brick wall after brick wall as the projected date for starting the publishing process drew closer. So, she wrote me a letter; heartfelt and filled with sincerity. She emphasized that our investors aren't coming through and we need to keep it moving instead of waiting for them to get their ducks in a row. She said the book was going to get published if she had to pay for it herself just to see the project to completion. My trust and faith in her in that instant grew stronger with what she was saying to me. Everyone that I thought would have my back were nowhere to be found. Potential initial investors were no longer answering the phones. Some of my family was tripping over the position Deidra was in, but she was all I had in my corner. I had to swallow my pride and let her help.

She was exactly the type of woman Junior and King said she was. Since this wasn't planned, she actually had to save this money little by little. The publication date got pushed back because of this but it was still progress to me. During this time, I learned much about other author options and requirements from her. Most importantly, I began to discover a masterpiece, a diamond in the rough so to speak. She shared snippets of her personal life with me along with some of her dreams and aspirations. Drama was the genre of her life but she was determined to rise above. I detected a rose that grew from concrete that perhaps just needed a little watering and fertilizer around the roots.

She was seeing someone at the time she told me. I remained silent about it and made it a point not to even broach the subject again. Whomever he was did not recognize what he had in my opinion. I saw the potential, ambition and real hunger for success and infrastructure in her life that she possessed.

I would often confide in her, pick her brain to see what she was really storing under her locks of hers that she often wore (per her admission) in a curly fro-type style. She was a natural-haired woman. She was different than women I had encountered in my lifetime. I've dealt with many along the many states of the east coast and across racial lines. She possessed something that they didn't. She knew her place in the earth as a woman. She could get my attention on any subject coming from a submissive place. She can be the boss without the bravado that a lot of women now have in trying to be the boss. She was not moved by material things, which I've encountered in dealing with gold diggers. Her nature was much like a humanitarian. I saw her as a woman destined to rewrite history with the right opportunity.

I was going to be patient and allow time to resolve this matter about "him". I discerned this woman had the characteristics I look for to be my future mate. I told her about my case, the times surrounding my conviction, and ultimately my vision for release. I also told her about the covenant I made with Yahweh. We exchanged business ideas from day on about a bartering system needed along with marketing, mobility and organization to help launch an infrastructure for the community. She was far from the typical "welfare mentality" state of mind that I had encountered in a lot of black women that I've dealt with whom were often without direction or purpose for their life or their children's lives. She, like me, only sought to have the opportunity to improve her situation.

When I was able to aid in any way, she'd always say "thanks" or "I appreciate it!" Nothing less. Nothing more. She was not one to convey her thoughts and intentions with use of much emotion. This was different for me. She was as simple and down to earth as it gets. At one point in time I got it in my mind I would help her or more like push her to get a car that she needed as the one she was driving was on the way out. I was able to find one for her through some networking and told her she should go check it out. She took down the information but was hesitant to go because as she put it, she did not want to go back to paying a car note every month. She went to check out the car I found for her but ended up driving home in another car that had more space and more doors. She said she probably would not have gone if it wasn't for me, but she is still happy with her purchase. She thanked me for my efforts in only a way she can.

She had a tendency to rip away the ego and machismo I often possessed. Something that I've learned about myself since dealing with Deidra is that my problem was the fact that I always sought the high maintenance women in the past.

Typically, the gold diggers, she taught me that the size of a woman's behind, sexual prowess or skin tone has absolutely nothing to do with the true nature of a woman. Through lengthy phone conversations by phone and lots of letters, I've discovered a paradigm. Love doesn't have a face. Loyalty doesn't come with butt size or physical appearance. It is the condition of the heart that reveals the most.

CHAPTER FIVE

When my oldest daughter tried to pull rank and sabotage my pursuit of this mission with Deidra, I wasn't having it.

She felt as if having Deidra's picture in my book was too much. She advised against it and I refused to have any more dealings with her as a result. My race to success didn't come with fanfare from family or anyone else close to me. It came from the person that was on this journey with me. I advise people to stick with who's sticking with them be it blood or not. Love doesn't pay any bills and family who opposes obtainable success for me is family best left behind. Family has been permitted to destroy millions of opportunities under the guise of sharing the same blood. We have to sometimes step away from the traditional definition of family overlooking the blood relation in favor of the organic family that propels us forward and elevate our way of living even though there is no relation by blood.

It's about fulfillment of dreams and obtaining goals with or without a family. I love my family unconditionally and would rather share in my accolades with them. However, choosing between them and the work I'm doing with Deidra is a decision I didn't toil over because I knew what I needed to do. People are going into the grave behind this warped perception of love broke, depressed, never creating or owning anything they built themselves. The world belongs to "reachers". Deidra is a reacher and very ambitious, like myself.

The simplest connection can cause your dreams and visions to be birthed into the world. Poverty and life's obstacles are nothing but stepping-stones or motivation for you to become creative, ambitions and a risk taker. It is during these times you most need to seek out opportunities. They're everywhere. What causes most individuals not to prosper in spite of their circumstances could be a multitude of things like prejudice or bias, depression due to their situation, pride, or having a fear of failure. It would be hard for them to become encouraged to take a chance and even more so when they listen to the wrong people.

I was terrified of failure when Deidra wrote me in response to a question I'd ask her along these lines. She said she wasn't afraid to take this risk and go along with me on this adventure but she does know what it meant to be afraid. She had tried many home-based businesses in which she done in her free time after school and/or work. They all failed but she learned from them. Timing is key! Plus, she stated that she didn't have the mindset then that she had now and felt that we could make this a success.

I could have kissed her feet at that moment when I read her letter. She was positive even with her inexperience in this particular venture. Being negative and doubtful is what holds a lot of us back. Your circumstances aren't the problem, it's being complacent with where you are and not taking the risks necessary to change it. As the singer Jon Legend says, we're all just ordinary people. Taking a leap of faith is what separates some from the rest. The person that wants something but does nothing gets nothing.

I went through hell to find Deidra. I was willing to go through more to keep her. If I were to leave this world, she would get everything I'm worth. She will divide what's left for my family amongst them and whoever chooses not to be a team player won't be playing. Blood isn't stronger than loyalty, especially when those claiming to be family and love you are disloyal. Deidra opened my eyes to something that's been plaguing the black community for a long time. We talk about loyalty but we're not being about it.

CHAPTER SIX

In my lifetime, I've admittedly been a manipulator and con artist, especially when it comes to loving a woman. If it was a course of study, I would have had my Master's and PhD in psychology of seducing a woman just to get between their legs. That is the shameful truth. I married two beautiful women. One in particular, named Michelle. I really owe her a public apology. (I'm truly sorry!). I was cheating within a year of the marriage like a lot of husbands and wives today. I also owe an apology to Angel. I should never have married her in this prison because it ended with her hating me. I was much like the average male today that are testosterone and ego driven. I was still a boy trying to fill a man's shoes.

In my youth, a man named George, from New York, told me that women were nothing more than "cum catchers" (excuse my language). This was the worst comment an older gray-haired man could ever make to an impressionable young adolescent. Although, watching the way most women I encountered degrade themselves in some form or fashion throughout my life made it easy to believe. It seemed that the standards were low as well as the expectations from women towards men. Most women have at least once given herself to a relationship with a male with no structure or moral support to offer them. They stopped demanding marriage before intimacy not realizing this is one of the more degrading and damaging things they can do to themselves. This present day is a reflection of it as the single parent home is of a higher percentage than it used to be.

A man is most animalistic until he reaches a point of maturity, especially as they relate to women. His lower nature is like a beast loose in the night. He has many faces and means of approach. What he says to a woman, regardless of how sweet and innocent it sounds, is usually fueled by his testosterone and/or obvious erection. Only women familiar with the tricks men pull can detect it.

CHAPTER SEVEN

I didn't detect a sense of lustfulness or vulgarity in her soul. She even admonished me about my sex scenes in my book. She commented that it was too explicit and I needed to change it. My first thoughts were, "Who does she think she is demanding me to alter the scenes in my book?" But then I remembered Proverbs 31: 10-31 about the virtuous woman. (You can read it for yourself). I believe she was sent by Yahweh to be the cleanser of my dark soul. I went back through my story and removed the hardcore scenes.

I threw away about five of what I think would have been best sellers. I felt they weren't fit for Deidra's eyes as my editor and agent. For the first time in my life, I'd met a woman in whom it mattered to me deeply what she thought and how she viewed me. I was trying to change at the core to form into a man of integrity, honor, and respect towards females. It felt supernatural to me. She handled me with truthfulness knowing that by and large, I was raised in the streets.

She has proven to be a great listener. She talks very little unless she has something on her mind or it's a subject she feels passionate about. She often says she can express herself more through writing rather than talking. When she talks, it's not like most women I've talked to that carry a sexual or seductive overtone in their voice. It was and still is mostly monotone with very little inflection.

CHAPTER EIGHT

I've extended to her what I felt was her worth. I called her "Sacred". I told her this is how I saw her as pure and untouched. I wrote it in a letter and ended it with a poem. After some conversation about it, she just said "okay". Although, she didn't agree in a literal sense, she accepted that I do hold her in high regard. Women and men must realize that a man has power to direct a woman to majesty, splendor and glorification or he can cause her to lower her self-respect and standards just to get what he wants from her. Sadly, the latter is the case for most males today.

This journey, however, has not been a walk in the park for me in getting to learn her. Her shy nature made her somewhat resistant and maybe cautious as well but that's to be expected initially. It was my burden to prove I can be trusted and not running "prison game". I displayed my huge trust in her with an exclusive power of attorney contract and doing my best to keep my word. I told her often I wish to make her a rich woman with this endeavor. I believe a man is a man based upon his potential and abilities not his surroundings or present dilemma. This woman had unknowingly saved my life and was in the process of fulfilling my dreams.

It takes a special person to look beyond the cage that is the correctional institution and see a human being. Especially, when it's someone not related to or familiar with you. The world at large had turned its back on me and forgot my name. I was a dead man to society, my peers, siblings and other members of my family who loved me with their words but not with action. They loved me with their lips but their hearts were far from it. My friend Joseph Hymen was the exception. He was a person I can talk too and confide in.

I've actually had a number of chicks interested in dating me until they discovered my sentence and how long life without parole really was. It was too long of a wait for them. I have paid bills for some even behind prison walls because I'm good at networking to get things done. The men they were dating did nothing. The worst part is that the women allowed this behavior. It's usually the standard for women that are drunk off a man's penis and the orgasms he gives her. Women are off balance in today's society. Everything is physical. If you remove sex out of the relationship, a lot of them will crumble due to not having a solid foundation based on attributes outside of the carnal nature.

CHAPTER NINE

Intimacy in America is distorted and overemphasized. In its present condition, it's bad for the brain. Sexual intercourse is supposed to be mainly for reproduction purposes and reassuring the bond between husband and wife. When a woman sleeps with a man outside of the sacredness of marriage, she has absolutely nothing to solidify his loyalty, commitment, or respect for her. It's difficult enough to salvage healthy relationships in marriages. It's reasonably harder when there is nothing but a sexual outlet. At least in a marriage the man tends to be not as easily straying due to running the risk of losing half his assets or having to pay alimony and/or child support. Some men still do, but it's just not the majority. I realized the error of my ways in my past marriages along this journey.

When I say Deidra saved my life and gave me reason to live. I'm not referring to just existing; it's only existing if it doesn't go beyond the basics of life (food, shelter, healthcare, etc.). Deidra fulfilled my dreams from prison. I'm a successful published author. My face and name rings around the world. I'm also a recognized poet since my recognition at the Kennedy Center program they have for incarcerated poets, authors, and playwrights. I am working towards my dream of owning a bondsman company as well as a real estate business because of her as I currently sit in prison (as of the writing of this book). She's used talents given to her by the Most High and those she's acquired over the years to help bring my first dream to fruition. She knows just as I do the value of being economically free. I am enabled to possibly give birth to the rewriting of penology and the process of reformation in prison.

Very few inmates have accomplished such mobility and organization from prison. This is what I mean when I say she has caused me to live and not just exist. The ideas were lying dormant inside of me. I needed someone selfless and smart enough to look deeper than the shell, as well as wise and open-minded enough to embrace my entrepreneurial insights. Women who focus mainly on a man's outward person or his present situation are often judgmental and disdaining, often miss the most astounding person and adventure they could have ever experienced. It's also fair to state that those same things may also be indicative of future failings as well depending on the circumstances.

The purpose of a man in a woman's life is to bring about a social and economic liberation status in which she doesn't just merely survive but thrives and cause their children to do the same.

CHAPTER TEN

A man is defined by his ability to shape the world, at least a piece of it anyway. Women should look to date a man that brings complete restoration to their life not wreck it. I had a female tell me that she didn't appreciate me pointing out the flaws in her man because she "loves" him. I said try telling that to Duke Power, the doctor or the cashier at the grocery store when she goes to buy food. Love does not pay any of those bills which affected her livelihood, so she would be advised to call her man to task or simply raise her standards for the next guy.

I offered a few of these women the same opportunity I presented to Deidra, but she was the only one open minded enough to jump on it. Also, others had boyfriends that stood in their way of progress. They're still broke today and don't show any desire to change their situation. Simply relying on one's ability to chase a wage (i.e. job) can leave you destitute in situations of emergency and/or job loss. Women being comfortable with living paycheck to paycheck with nothing but a penis and bills not paid to show for it have their standards set on "low". You are worth so much more!

Those that don't know the difference in living and not just existing typically are the ones just existing. Even from prison, I have made it my duty to not just be a number in a system. Prison is a mental institution for the insane and if you aren't when you arrive within these walls lie circumstances that will drive you in that direction. However, it is like a Harvard college for the man who thinks outside the box. It is the breeding ground for writers and a variety of artists like me. Thanks to Deidra now there is a face to go with the name Robert Graham, Jr. a.k.a. "Yahborn".

She is a true humanitarian like myself. She's not condescending or controversial and treats me with respect. I would have never thought a woman of her caliber would consider dealing with someone like me be it business or otherwise. I have learned from her about purity of the heart and mind as well as raw honesty as it relates to a woman. She likes to point to the "Golden Rule" when asked why she thoughtful of others. "Do unto others as you would have them do unto you". I think we would as people treat each other better if we got the return on our actions almost immediately.

Never have I trusted a woman with my weaknesses and shameful things of my past. Talking and confiding in her made me vulnerable and as transparent as glass. I have the deep sense inside that she's not judging me and she understands. Guilt and condemnation would normally torment my soul when dealing with others that listened only to respond with scolding words. She proved to me that she felt I was worth her time and investment because she sacrificed when she didn't have to. It made it easier for me to put her in charge of everything.

I had put my life into a woman's hands that I haven't even seen face-to-face. I was walking by faith not by sight. My discernment and in depth conversations with her assured me that she was "the real McCoy". When I told her that I trusted her with my life and my trust was unconditional. She sighed and grew completely silent over the phone. She was completely taken aback. "Hello?!" I called out. She replied that she was still on the phone but what I said kind of caught her off guard.

She replied that she thought that was too much trust and that being in this position sounded like a lot of responsibility to have on one's shoulders. However, she already had begun the process and was not about to opt out now. She was one that liked to finish what she starts. I asked her if she could handle it. To which she simply replied with laughter and a simple yes.

CHAPTER ELEVEN

Trusting a woman with your life is something not too bizarre when you're married. However, to give such trust to a woman you have never seen and have only communicated with via phone and mail is like something one would see in a movie. Absolute peace flooded my soul about the matter despite the fact that I had done something I swore I would never ever do. I swore I wouldn't trust any woman especially, unconditionally. I felt that there was something supernatural guiding this venture and despite my initial reservations I was now excited to see what this journey would bring.

After dealing with multitudes of women I finally came across one who was official. She was certifiably true to her word. She didn't do much without consulting me first even though I let her know I trusted her judgment. She felt it necessary to include me since the book was my body of work. I've encountered many women who often overstep their bounds and I was waiting to see if she would do the same to no avail. I felt she was being used by Yahweh to teach me about loyalty. I've been blessed with a lot of talents in my life, but loyalty wasn't one of them.

When a mature woman steps into a man's life she can provide incentive for him to reach his apex. I just wonder where I'd be if Deidra had not taken a chance on me. If she had the mindset against aiding and assisting me like most females in society, it would have been devastating me. She also would have missed out on the opportunity to expand her horizons and increase her own knowledge base. Lucky for me she took the risk. This risk saved my life and fulfilled my dream. In society, people are always judging prisoners by our past, as if they can see into our future. I've yet to see a crystal ball.

The first time I asked Deidra if she believed we could complete this mission, she replied with a simple "yes". She said she not only believed in us but also in me. She meant it too. The validation was exactly what I needed to fight past all the damage the South Carolina Department of Corrections had done to my psychological well-being. Her words became stronger and more impactful than any negative or demeaning things prison had to offer. Inside I felt I was rising taller than a mountain.

CHAPTER TWELVE

I felt like I was alive again, not just existing. I had a reason to live and not just go along with business as usual. I had a whole new outlook on life and it wasn't through the eyes of the penal institution. If she believed in me, that's all I needed to hear. It brought the vividness back to my mentality. I was no longer angry at officers and didn't care if they acted like hypocrites or didn't respect me. What mattered is that I respected me and that I loved myself. My life didn't seem to be lost in this judicial system or it's process of demonization of those incarcerated thanks to Yahweh and the gift of belief from this woman. I surmised that it was not my fault if the people of the world didn't see a reason to be civil towards me. I consider it their loss not mine.

I wanted to experience more growth so that means I needed to be held accountable for the plans I set forth or the actions I took. Making Deidra my accountability partner just made sense. However, this was not as easy for me because that would mean I would have to be vulnerable before her. I wanted to be an authentic man at all costs so I went for it. Unbeknownst to me she was familiar with what an accountability partner was and stated she is one to someone that is also hers. They kept each other on tasks with achieving their goals in pursuit of their dreams and life milestones. She also agreed to be mine as well. I definitely wanted to prove myself to be someone worth taking the risk for that she did in coming along this journey with me.

An accountability partner is one who divulged your entire being to if you really want to experience true growth. I shared things from 12 years of age until my present age of 48. Your partner will not only prevent you from making the wrong choices, but also keep you alert in knowing what to look for in life, people, situations, etc. that can be helpful or harmful. They are like a divining rod.

It is important that the selection of your accountability partner is not taken lightly. You can't pick yes-men or yes-women. That defeats the purpose. This person must care for your life and want you to achieve success in what you do. Don't make it someone you are not comfortable with so you are not afraid to be open, but at the same time don't pick anyone you are too comfortable with, as you may not respect his or her corrective advice. You can have multiple accountability partners. You may have one for personal accountability while you have a different one for work or business goals. You will experience more growth the more transparent you are with them. They can't advise you on things you don't tell them about or give a complete assessment without knowing the all the important details. Respect and some experience in the area you need accountability should also be taken into account. It will allow you to trust the advice you're given more as well as be able to rely on the fact that it comes from a solid source.

For me, it was like having a non-biased person to talk with about my promiscuous past. I also talked about how even now my mind leads me to try to pursue these high maintenance females for relationships. Don't think that prison bars ever stopped a man from pursuing a woman or vice versa. After discussing it, with my accountability partner, I did realize that this is something I should not do provided it had led to nothing but strife and downfall in my past. I come to realize that I should only allow certain females in my company that meet the standards and all others should be castaway or fed with a long spoon. Not doing so will only be a distraction that will take me off the path of bettering myself.

I had often encountered women who simply wanted intimate relations with no possibility of marriage, little to no morals or self-esteem, and also no knowledge of self or about our history as a people. They were filled with attitude and lack a compassionate, humanitarian type spirit. None of that would be conducive to the person I am trying to be.

Typically, people have accountability partners that are the same gender as them as it may avoid complication that may arise in male-female interactions. There is no flirting or illicit behavior at all in my accountability partnership because of the type of person Deidra is. She is not the type to use her feminine wilds to persuade or influence to act in her own self-interest over others. I've had women try to come at me like that even while incarcerated, but Deidra is the first female that I have come across that seems balanced enough to be in this position. She is not driven by her sexual prowess. She keeps it professional and courteous.

CHAPTER THIRTEEN

In one of her letters of correspondence to me, Deidra wrote in regards to some issues within our community that black males need opportunity, incentives and an outlet for expression. I found this to be profound to how she was in tuned with what young black men needed even though she was a black woman. She is a mother to a young black male she is raising on her own but she has managed to get him through life and off to college without any major traps that hit her brothers in their adult life. Even as a mom of a son, I've found that most females can't see past their gender to have empathy for the trials and tribulations of their own male son. That makes her stand out to me.

I thought the concept of her statement was reflective of her intellect and awareness. I had to meditate on it. Women all over the world are engaging with males on many different levels from being mothers, sisters, friends, and significant others. Yet you don't see many of them empower the male to rule his own destiny. They may date, marry and/or have babies by them but these men are just existing in relationships and not ruling or rooted in a structure he himself has created for them both.

The potential of a man is quite often brought out or inspired by a woman or cause that he holds most sacred. A woman, in tuned with the core of her womanhood has the ability to see the potential that may lie hidden inside. She's designed to nurture him and capture his attention on what his future purpose may be. This gift comes from the Creator.

I'm convinced that today's relationships are full of selfishness and self-righteousness, which disrupts the balance of both the male and female in the relationship. People have become so desperate for physical, momentary highs that they end up with the wrong mates. It is critical that women first look to what a man has contained within his mind and spirit.

Robert Graham Jr

In one of the letters I wrote to Deidra I shared at length on the fact that I was "pregnant". Pause! I know what you're thinking. Yes, I know men can't physically get pregnant. Figuratively I meant that I was filled with something that I felt I was about to give birth to. That "something", were my visions and dreams that I was in pursuit of to make come to fruition. I won't convey them all in this book but just know that this cage can't contain the purpose that lies inside my brain. She helped to revive that side of me.

When females can get their minds away from their carnal nature and the infatuation of just being in a relationship "just because", they can allow themselves to experience growth and development in character. They will also get more out of the relationships they participate in aside from the "romanticized" parts. These are the type of women who can help a man reach heights he ordinarily would not.

CHAPTER FOURTEEN

Women have at least four primary ways in which they normally communicate to a man their sincerest thoughts.

The first is verbal, the others are inflection of tone, things they don't say but you know they should and of course their body language. Being that I only communicated with Deidra through phone or letters, I could never read her body language and relying on the other forms was quite hard at first because she normally does more listening than talking. This is different from the norm for me in regards to women, so she was a bit difficult to read. When she did talk I learned to eventually get a read on the things she said and how she says them. I felt when she was attentively listening to a conversation or if I was saying something she may have a different view on. Once I understood her way, I no longer had my own expectations that I imposed on her that she would respond in a specific way to certain conversations.

There's also a tone in her voice that tells me how to and how not to relate to her on certain issues. She would also be slow or hesitant to converse fluidly when she has a difference of opinion. She almost never gives me unsolicited information in any regards. When we speak on topics she is passionate about the words start to flow like a stream. Since I couldn't read her body language though it did create a bit of an obstacle of me getting full comprehension from our dialogue. This relationship is not one solidified by physical assets but of clear meaningful conversation and noble actions. She is the first woman that I've known to really get my attention and keep it just based off her mental capacity.

She's not one to play games or send mixed signals. Most women I have come in contact with were not mature enough in their interactions with a man to communicate clearly to him with boundaries while also expressing her boundaries. She convinced me that I should consider writing an autobiography. I told her that I wasn't going to write it unless

I can include her in it. She agreed but also reiterated that an autobiography is supposed to be about one's own life. I told her that she was the catalyst for this life I am now living. Even though, I began to write it as I initially set out, after much deliberation and conversing back and forth, it soon became the inspiration for this book you are now reading. She enhanced my self-esteem, masculinity, creativity and the ability to feel like a free man. It's like the Creator sent me exactly what I needed to fuel all the things that will not only help me survive, but thrive into higher levels of achievement.

For her to allow me to include her in something that could be read worldwide means that she had some level of trust in me and was not concerned about our association or how society perceived it. My soul was being delivered from the stigmas and stereotypes commonly placed on the incarcerated.

CHAPTER FIFTEEN

Some people say LOVE is physical. They think that true love cannot exist without the touch from another's hands. At the same time, you don't see true love often spurring from "one night stands". What is love when people who say they have it has cheated once or twice or have been cheated on. They also lie to each other during the course of the relationship. People that often marry for love end up getting a divorce.

In today's society the focus lies on the material but mostly the physical. What about the part of love or loving someone that comes way before the intimacy? (or at least it should) How can you fulfill your partner other than through sexual relations?

If you look at the most prominent celebrity male, you may see him involved or "in love" numerous times yet being shrouded in love, sex nor wealth has made them stay faithful. Truth be told, the wealth is probably the gateway that provides people to cheat with. Also, women of today mistake love for sex when sex for a lot of males today have nothing to do with love in terms of an emotional connection. Women often end up in a heartbroken state confusing the two.

True love cannot be mostly tied to how a person looks. I'm sure you know tons of gorgeous celebrity men and women who can't seem to hold on to a significant other even when they marry. It is typically something in their character that is driving the other person away or causing them to select poor choices to begin with.

Love is deeper than a word you say to someone, acts of passion or emotions invoked. It is a union in which one balances out the other. It is living your life with the intent of fulfilling and enhancing the life of your significant other. Sex and marriage are like the extra toppings. We were taught a simplified version of what love is really like in elementary school by learning what's called "The Golden Rule". "Do unto others as you have them do unto you" is as plain as it gets. Deidra often refers to that rule a lot and exemplified it in her dealings with me. She accepted this opportunity to work with me even in this state I am in. I appreciate her generosity and kindness. If you want someone to be able to look beyond your faults and see your needs, you must be willing to do the same. The basics of love can also be found in 1 Corinthians 13: 4-8.

I wrote this book with intention to shed much needed light on some things from behind these prison walls. I only have Deidra in my life due to favor from Yahweh the Creator. In our lifetime most of us has squandered away our lives with an obsession or desperation of physical touch. We've done whatever it took to get it: to feed our addictions so to speak. My intentions are to get you to think and move beyond the carnal nature.

At this point in my life I am keenly aware of the cognitive dissonance that's enslaved the masses not only when it comes to love, but other issues as well.

CHAPTER SIXTEEN

When I proclaim that I love Deidra, I'm not referring to love that comes with lust. It is different.

When we first spoke, I noticed that the normal lust that I'd have towards a woman was waned. It wasn't there. My potential to engage in conversation that was vulgar or perverse in a sexual nature was nonexistent. In turn, my approach towards her wasn't physically based. Her conversations with me, did not awaken the god of lust or promiscuousness. She kept it plain and simple. Even when I requested a picture from her to put a face to the woman I was talking to, she sent a photo that was not revealing or sexually suggestive. I did find her to be beautiful though.

In her interactions with me I don't detect any flirtatiousness or lustful spirit. I know what to look for based on my experiences with other women before and after being behind bars. She was uniquely different. I made up my mind to show her the utmost respect and still continue to do so. After all, she did help save my soul through the mercy of Yahweh by keeping those sexual doors closed while in conversation and dealings with me.

Some women like to be exploited. This I have learned from my experiences. That's the only way they feel you love them, which is a flawed way of reasoning that exists today. I often tell Deidra she is like a virgin to me. She has a shy, humble nature about her. She's also not temperamental or condescending in the way that she talks to me. This empowered me to take my mind off her physicality and focus on her spiritually and socially. Plus, it also allowed me to honor her like a man is supposed to honor a woman. It was clear to me that lust was not at the center of her life. This allowed me to be engaged in other aspects of my life and most of all my purpose.

Before long, I found myself loving her without the testosterone or hormonal exertion. This is what I mean when I say that I love her. I confided in her with caution about this and what she's done for my life. To which she simply replied, "Well!" I'm glad that I'm able to help." I was amazed at how she exercised discipline and maturity in our relationship. This kept me determined not to mess it up. I kept it completely honest with her in exposing some of my old ways of being a womanizer, sexist and opportunist. She didn't mind my truthfulness. She is the first woman that I haven't told a lie to. This mere fact alone made her the perfect candidate to be my accountability partner.

When I had interactions with other females, I made her aware. It didn't matter if it was innocent or not, I just wanted to be honest with my accountability partner and keep her respect. She showed an interest in my growth and maturity that I set out to accomplish so I was interested in her feedback whether she agreed with my actions or not. This is the power of a woman and the reason a man is to want her, definitely not solely her outward appearance. The relationship is about growth and character development; these are the more valuable forms of a love you can give to a person.

This is a first for me to experience a relationship of this kind with a woman. Most of the ones I have experienced with a woman not in my family were based on lust. When consumed by lustful emotions, two people can't honor and appreciate each other's qualities and aid in each other's pursuit in life. The mind is always focused on self-pleasure. Having this mindset can often hinder or stop completely a person from elevating to the next level in life. Truth be told there are a good number of people, men especially! sitting in jail or prison behind the antics that came along with a lustful, nonproductive relationship. These relationships bear no fruit worth harvesting. There is no focus on establishing foundation for the current and next generations or leaving a blueprint for them to pattern after when they are long gone.

This is highly needed to change the course of a family and community's future. These are the types of conversations I am able to have with Deidra and she gets it. She is in agreement as these are also the kinds of things she discusses amongst her friends on social media as well she once told me. This is what gets me high about her and especially when we discuss helping to bring structure in the lives of others. It is a rarity to find someone in our community that you can have these kinds of discussions with and you don't find many behind these walls either.

A woman with organizational and investment strategies is worth lusting after versus one with enhanced assets and a narrow or unfruitful mindset. The same goes for a man. Enhancing the lives of your mate is something both should make a priority when entering a relationship.

I don't make light of the importance of intimacy at all in a sound mature relationship because it helps the bond grow stronger. The Creator made us for the gift of such a beautiful gift of being engulfed and intertwined flesh to flesh with each other. It is after all a method of procreation to grow our families and relational enhancement. The problem with the current state is that intimacy is exploited and out of order from its original intention.

CHAPTER SEVENTEEN

To me, Deidra is sacred. In fact, I actually call her that, "Sacred". I have such reverence and honor for her simply because of what she has done for me already. I tell her that she is royal, precious and divine in my eyes. She's the most important woman in this earth right now because of her position in my life and the position she has caused me to be in. Granted we are not in a dating relationship, I just really do hold her in high regard, even above my own mother and I love her dearly. I have defended her honor against those that try to impose be it friend or family member. They are now perfectly clear on where I stand with having her in my life.

When I say she's sacred, I'm not saying she is perfect because most have flaws and make mistakes. Women have the capacity to return to their innocence and purity. It only takes a decision to do so. The past does not have to always be the precedence at which someone's future is defined.

Speaking of defining things, I wish women would realize that sleaziness does not equate to prettiness or overall beauty. It is your natural beauty from the inside out that really attracts and keeps a mature man. In the days of my immaturity, I will admit I once thought that the ideal beauty was a red boned, longhaired honey with a coke bottle shape and naturally long hair. These were women I chased for a good time, but not married. Women need to learn to be confident and comfortable in the skin they are in and with what the Creator gave them from birth. Now this does not mean there shouldn't be any maintenance. Our bodies should be treated like a special temple because we only get one. Diet and exercise is key to healthy maintenance and good hygiene is also a must for us all.

In getting to know Sacred, as a person my past flawed preferences were exposed because she is the exact opposite of the types I used to go for. She enjoys being naturally her without all the extra fake accessories or bougie attitudes to match. She definitely took me to school and opened my eyes to some things. I was typically enticed by women with glamorous seduction, which often lead to relationships of being unequally yoked in mindsets and lots of drama. In today's society, you can see these types of women filling the pages of social media for attention, unfortunately. Leading with their looks and bodies but ultimately wondering why they are still all alone or just in short-lived relationships. It is wise for women to think on these things.

A man telling you how fine you look half naked is first trying to score. He is not thinking of having you around for something serious or long term.

CHAPTER EIGHTEEN

A woman is a man's mirror (and vice versa). The person we select as a mate often reflects our innermost workings or at least that's how it should be. A man receives his validation from his woman and often times when that's not the case, a man strays from the relationship. Our friends in our lives also serve as mirrors. These relationships tell a little about who you are as a whole. I see Sacred as one of those mirrors.

I remember in one of her letters she wrote that she felt 2015 would give birth to some great things, but was unsure of what they were. She stated that if it was progress in the right direction, she was happy for it. I too had that same feeling in my spirit so it caused me to pay close attention. I felt that we were on one accord and she would be willing to support me in the fulfillment of all my dreams and visions as long as they were positive. Before this point I was hesitant to divulge to her my endeavors I would like to explore for the future. Every other black woman I had encountered was so blinded and scornful towards my being in prison and the length of my sentence so I assumed her to have the same mindset.

I'm glad I was wrong. She was a visionary all on her own and understood the possibility of pursuing visions or dreams. I had actually started along this path towards my endeavors many times with other females. They were unable to see the possibility in my visions. They couldn't see me but Deidra did see that I was purpose driven to say the least. That's all I needed to know to begin to make adjustments in several areas of my life.

A man doesn't need to be a student at Harvard or Martin Luther King, Jr. to have a world-changing dream, be brilliant or resourceful. They have to have Coretta Scott Kings or Michelle Obamas to have their back and support them. Where are they in this "independent woman" society? These were strong, powerful women in their own rite but they never tried to overshadow or stand in the way of their mate in the pursuit of their goals.

A woman has the power to provoke a man to rule. As I told Sacred, a man is placed on this earth to bring about order, mobility and infrastructure. When a woman shifts the focus from a sexual nature to a mental one, she has the ability to ensure that his value system and focus is intact. When addressing his weaknesses or shortcomings she does it in a way that does no damage to his psyche. She makes certain that she presents herself to him in such a way that he's comfortable and feels free enough to discuss anything with her. In the end, we all have struggles, but knowing and admitting what they are is half the battle to conquering them.

CHAPTER NINETEEN

I believe that it was a supernatural occurrence that Sacred was placed in my life to spearhead this movement and adventure that I planned to embark on. Her belief that 2015 would spark great things was confirmation enough for me. It opened my eyes towards her being the strategic answers to my prayers. There was something much deeper to her and I could sense that. My life has typically been filled with prophetic words from people and I felt deep inside she was right.

However, I felt I had to test her faith, maturity, and breadth of wisdom. I thought that there was no way she could have spoken something so profound that I resonated with unless she was the one I was waiting for to help me along this journey. I did a little acid test. I watched and observed to see any signs that she would become a liability to me. I looked for her behavior to change as in prideful or conceited in any way. For months I gave her free reign to act on my behalf without consulting me as long as it was within the confines of our contracts and discussions. She only needed to consult with me of her decisions after she had made them. She wouldn't bite. She simply said she could not do it completely because it was my project but she appreciated the faith and trust that I had in her. It eased her consciousness to consult with me to make sure it is in line with what I wanted. I came to the conclusion she was officially who she claims to be.

I let up for a couple of months then I presented her with it again. I had already anticipated that she wouldn't take the bait. I just needed to satisfy negative thoughts the enemy and family members that were upset by the amount of trust I put into someone I haven't met had put into my head. This time was different because I was serious. I wanted her to assume absolute decision making over not just my business but whatever assets remained after I was gone. This was sure to force her hand, but I felt she was more than capable, and I wanted to see if the pressure would cause her to crumble or produce a diamond. To make a long story short, she's still shining brightly.

Her task was to perform as if I had left the earth because upon my release I have personal plans for myself and would not be able to be as hands on as I would like to. She would be the brains and mouthpiece for us both. Having her take on this task was probably one of the most profitable and wise decisions I'd ever make that included a woman. She already had a similar thought pattern and decision-making pattern as I did so it seemed like a no brainer at this point. She would make an excellent business partner.

As it stood, I got to observe her make decisions towards this project we were embarking on and in the different aspects required. She proved to me she could handle being in control and the power I had bestowed upon her. She is the brains behind my success thus far. This is the true power and purpose of a woman in a man's life.

CHAPTER TWENTY

People have their own views one way or another on what's proper in relationships and it's all somewhat programmed by societal influences and agendas. The lines have often been blurred in between what's acceptable and what's not. It used to be that having multiple partners while in a relationship was deemed as cheating. Now it's open relationships (even marriages), threesomes and an abundance of swing parties in which couples swap partners. We also have same sex relationships along with gender swapping and confusion. These days we don't appear to notice the difference between male and females when it comes to cohabitation. Standards and logic or common sense have been overlooked if not completely missing. It is just a ball of confusion out here.

Times have changed. Women are consciously opting to have babies without fathers for them. They are also having multiple children that end up having multiple fathers without any backlash or recourse for the situations they have created. You find this behavior even among women claiming to be Christian and they are associated with jokes of being the biggest freaks. This was definitely not the case back in the day. You got an earful if you ever came at them with any type of disrespect.

Today, women approach the males with sensual advances. The difference from right and wrong has been intertwined to suit agendas. It's pure madness. Building a solid foundation amidst a mess is almost impossible which is why one must cling to what is sound and stable when they find it.

CHAPTER TWENTY-ONE

My goal is to shine a light and bring validation to the capability of a woman rooted in her true nature in the earth. Obviously I cannot touch on every subject as that would make the book too long, but I have made a concerted effort at attempting to enlighten one about a woman's capacity and true purpose beyond the physical, shallow agendas society continues to push. I felt it was a must that I write about this but also include Deidra ("Sacred") as an example on some points.

She changed a lot of my views in regards to women. I used to always judge them based off of what I've experienced and treat them accordingly. She set a new standard for me. Her courage, faith and vitality to sow into my dreams and visions with the utilization of her time and talent is brave and praiseworthy. My thought process in disclosing this experience is to show the possible in situations society has mostly deemed impossible but most importantly show how woman has the power to influence and empower a man to do the impossible. No, I don't recommend women to look to the prisons for men they can empower. That's not what I'm promoting. However, I will tell you that men that have untapped potential to do great things are confined to these penal institutions just as they are walking free amongst you. They are also not just spouses or potential spouses, but they are also brothers and sons.

I apologize to you women whom society has bred to pursue love and happiness in a man, before discovering our potential and base your decisions solely on our physical and other shallow inclinations. I feel sorry for you women who've only became infatuated by sharing or feeding on a man's spotlight and riches instead of focusing on finding your own greatest achievement and lacking the capacity to take hold of a man's heart and spirit that empowers you as you empower him. Ladies you've missed your original purpose or status if all you've provided incentive for your man to do is work on a job and bring you money or simply give you sex and children. You're meant for so much more than that.

Ask a man about his dreams. Engage him in thought provoking conversation. Replace his physical lust over your looks and assets with admiration and respect from what's in your mind and your heart. If at this stage you lack the capacity to do so, I suggest you take the time to take your own personal quest for growth and maturity.

CHAPTER TWENTY-TWO

From my teenage years, I've always carried a deep thought that a woman largely has the capacity of saving a man's life spiritually, socially, and physically. Many times I've tried to find such a woman that could possibly match my ability and my mindset. Many failed, obviously. A woman must be a willing participant. Her will is as strong as ten horses. What she doesn't choose to do of her own volition does not get done. It is wise for a man to not waste his time there. I've learned this lesson more than a hundred times to a fault. For a man trying to accomplish or build anything with a woman ignorant of her true worth and value is the equivalent of like an eagle trying to soar without wings.

I've tried with women of all types, especially those with a body like Beyoncé. They weren't visionaries like a Michelle Obama, just carnal minded females with a focus on the here and now rather than the future. They prefer the microwave approach rather than the slow bake that ensures things are properly done. It is a problem when women spend more time putting on makeup, shopping, and hanging out than she does her own personal development and growth. She is going to be void of a leading woman's essentials to transition to the next level.

In my experience, I've found a different mindset between women up north like New York and women in the south. Women from the south don't seem to know what they want beyond a job and the usual and they tend to not get too much outside of their comfort zone. Up north is where you find a lot of the go-getters but it could be because of how city life has this "only the strong survive" type of feel.

I've not encountered that until I met Sacred. She had the adventurous, spiritual, social and relational qualities I saw in women up north. They always have their game face on and ready to go for broke to achieve success. One such as myself, would not have to beg them to take interest in my plight.

They're risk-takers! My issue was that I was too homesick and missing my mom, so it was back down south for me. Even though nothing flourished, business wise, I did acquire much more fundamental enlightenment about life and my purpose since that time.

However, I did have some trace patterns of the above mentioned behavior and mindset. Coming in contact with a woman like Sacred helped me work my way through the residual ways that remained. A man often has many battles to overcome in order to rise to the standard of man he's supposed to be. It helps to have someone who can help keep him accountable. If you think about it, great men fall all the time and often without warning behind dealings with a woman. A man's weakness told to the wrong woman can take him down just as fast as he rises. By that same token, in the hands of the right woman he can work his way through to overcome them. Women with proper mindsets and maturity can be a valuable lifeline to a man who's figuratively on life support. I was blessed by Yahweh for using Sacred to save my life by giving me a renewed spirit and the achievement of my dreams.

I became a womanizer and a ladies' man from time of losing my virginity to a much older woman at the age of 19. I disclosed all this to my accountability partner because I know currently and upon my release, the biggest test will come from woman. I asked her to help keep me accountable so I don't make any decisions that will be the undoing of what I've accomplished so far and a hindrance upon my release. When I told her, I expected her to be somewhat jealous or offended but she was neither. She just laughed and assured me that she can help me in that area. Most women I've encountered would have been in their feelings about the matter. Sacred is not like that at all, she definitely has more of a professional interest than anything. She's definitely comfortable in her own skin and not about the drama nor thirsty for attention.

CHAPTER TWENTY-THREE

Keep it honest. Often when a man lies to a woman, it strikes a chord with her that he doesn't trust her response. He fears she may leave him or think small of him. Women sometimes make a stupid and costly decision when she belittles her mate. She breaks his confidence to confide in her completely. I find that the more a man honors a woman, the more he will refrain from lying to her or bringing shame and embarrassment to the relationship.

When a woman doesn't comprehend how to respond to a man's struggles, she's telling him that she's unworthy of him bothering to confide in her. For the first time in my life I have found a woman that I can tell everything to without being afraid of her response. Its established an open line of communication beyond what I can convey on paper. She mostly listens and gives her input without the judgement or condescending nature I've experienced before. It's important for two people to have this with each other in any kind of relationship they may have on a personal level.

I will tell you firsthand, that it is a dynamic experience. One of the biggest reasons men often confide in women that are considered strangers to them is the fact that they don't feel an explosion of emotions is likely to happen like with their significant other. You tend to get less judgement from people that don't readily know you or think they know you.

This often happens when people choose the wrong mates as I've stated before. Being tied to someone who's not the perfection or completion of you is akin to an eagle trying to soar without wings. It very well may still be an eagle. However, even though it was created to fly it can simply just walk around because it lacks the capacity to fly. Being attached to the wrong mate can clip your wings and limit your potential. That goes for both men and women. Lying to a woman is something I know all about due to my past ways of living.

I have obtained many wounds from the lies I told to different women. I used to be a great liar. I could look a woman straight in her eyes without blinking and deliver them like UPS delivers your mail. Men aren't going to be able to just lie to a woman who holds herself in high esteem and sacredness. She would rather be alone than be subjected to a life of untruths. Frankly, if the one you're with is a liar, you are already alone in some way in the relationship. One can't allow themselves to be blinded by the others physical or sexual being. Where lying begins, the destiny of that relationship comes to an end. Lies often corrupt a person spiritually and mentally.

As a womanizer, often what the women learned about me was rooted in lies, schemes and manipulation. That's why those relationships never really lasted. When two people are afraid and reluctant to be transparent, their souls nor their hearts will not completely mesh. We lie sometimes out of fear of rejection or being hurt. Two mature people can still bring each other to the point of freely expressing one's thoughts and feelings without fear of consequence or shame.

When two hearts become one the lies should cease. Traditionally and maybe even culturally, we assume that just because two people take vows and pledge allegiance to each other that their hearts are one. This is flawed thinking as seen by the rate of divorce that exists in this country. The majority of relationships have been infiltrated by lies, betrayal, adultery, and secrets that will dissolve their marriage if they were exposed.

It's important that the foundation of any relationship has a root in the truth. I made it clear to Sacred that I will not lie to her and that she should not lie to me because it will cause me to lose trust in her. I shared with her my struggle about an issue in which I had allowed someone really close to me to believe something that was not true. I explained to her that it was bothering me, and I gave

Robert Graham Jr

58

her my heartfelt spill on how devastating revealing the truth about the matter would be to this person. She didn't beat around the bush. She just told me it was deception plain and simple. She said I should be honest with that person regardless cause it would be more hurtful if they found out through someone else. She was right, although I felt reluctant about this situation. You have to have an accountability partner that will call you to the carpet to do the hard stuff. That's how you grow!

CHAPTER TWENTY-FOUR

At some point in our lives we must go where it's uncomfortable in order to grow. We must take the risks and remove the restraints we place on our minds and hearts. In order to experience this thing called love, sometimes you have to just be vulnerable and raw but with the right person of course. I took oaths and made vows long ago, that I was never going to fall in love with anyone's daughter. People claim to have been in love all around the world, but many don't even know the true meaning of the word.

When in true love, it's like this person really has dominion over your soul. You follow them to the ends of the earth. This kind of love can be found in a lot of elderly couples. When one of them passes it's like the life force from the other one remaining wants to follow and sometimes it eventually does. They were connected and essentially one. It's rare to find that kind of love thriving these days where souls join permanently.

People lie boldly even when they say the word to each other. They tell their significant other while lying and cheating with other people. I think we have this programmed or spoon fed idealism of what love means involving a lot of things that doesn't scratch the surface or reach the depth of what it really means. It's often associated with a physical thing, feeling or an image.

The world has never given an accurate description of it. We typically base it off strong emotions and feelings towards each other. A lot of relationships are formed by looks and physical pleasures of some kind, if not financial dependence. Most people just are selfishly in love. Lovers of themselves first before the ones they claim to love. Real love isn't selfish. The concept is bigger than how we feel. Feelings and emotions come and go like ships in the night.

CHAPTER TWENTY-FIVE

One of Sacred's most valuable qualities that she possesses is her praying for me. Although, I was the one who suggested it. However, she did not oppose. I'm left in awe just by listening and capturing her choice of words, which are not flowery, or dramatic by the way. She speaks what is in her heart and mind to speak. I often ask her to pray over me if I'm struggling with a major decision or just needing to be at peace.

This is another aspect to the power of a woman. Her prayers are soothing and liberating to my soul. Her voice works wonders for providing guidance and momentum from Yahweh to forge ahead on the journey and excel. I trust the purity of her heart.

It is an asset for a man to have a praying woman in their life and likewise for a woman to have a praying man. It fills the inspirational/spiritual aspect of their relationship whatever type it may be. Having this between the two can empower one or both to overcome obstacles and will bring strong unity between the parties involved. I typically feel bolder and more confident afterwards.

This has increased my spiritual growth as well. Through letters and conversations, she has helped me figure a lot of things out using her logical approach which in turned helped me get a better picture of things to see them more clearly. This reduced some of the spiritual fogginess bringing truth and validation. She's equipped to handle any question I ask coming from a spiritual, social or emotional perspective.

She's not close minded to learning new things but is careful as to the things her brain digests. She does her own research on information presented if it's something she is not familiar with and reconciles it with what makes sense to her logically.

She's more logic minded than anything else which is what I found different than most women. She will provoke you to think and research yourself with the information she presents. She has surprised me with the wealth of knowledge she has numerous times and I love her for that trait. We must grow and learn from one another because iron sharpens iron.

CHAPTER TWENTY-SIX

I've tried to outline the most meaningful and noticeable impact Sacred has had on my life. I was thankful she detected something in me much greater than just an urban novel writer. I was able to feel comfortable confiding in me about all the things I felt that were the dark parts of me. She remained the same as she was before I revealed things to her. For the first time in my life I felt a bit ashamed and not up to par.

I call her Sacred because it is true. Initially, I didn't start out with this high grade of respect for her. The way she carried herself and her temperament passively demanded and earned it. A man truly knows a woman he can respect and one he can get away with disrespecting just as a woman can bring greatness or death and/or destruction out of a man. Many has started out on this journey called life. Consequently, a lot have grown to be bitter, resentful and angry about how their life has turned out. Some may have been taken for a ride or bamboozled in a sense. Some have broken hearts because of lies and deceit. These situations are not new and at the very least one has to stop and acknowledge that through it all they are still here.

Like me, you must not be afraid to play the cards life dealt you. Depending on the cards a man is dealt, the right woman can provide the cards he needs to create a winning hand. However, this man must not be afraid to do so. A scared man can never really become great. He would be too afraid to challenge the odds. A woman must not be a scornful woman, this does nothing to encourage growth. Many become that way due to their past experiences in life or with wrong men that they chose. It is best to learn how to leave things in the past when dealing with present and future people. It's not to say that lessons should never be learned from past experiences, but the same negative emotions and behaviors should not be unleashed on others you may meet who had nothing to do with the situation. However, be advised that if you keep choosing the same situations, people, etc. you are more than likely to get the same outcome.

The thing I liked about Sacred is that she was not like that. She had a different understanding than most females I had come across. She understood history, struggles and the social programming the black community has undergone and how it has affected both females and males alike. There are generations of societal programming that is contributing to our downfall and really the downfall of mankind. It is important that both understand the gravity of the situation   at hand when dealing with one another.

Leaving the past in the past, allows us to not block opportunities and blessings when they are presented. Had Sacred, done that I would not be able to bring you this book or others. She's extremely knowledgeable and usually always one step ahead of me. She understood that many of us did not leave that breeder mentality on the plantation. We have a hint of the breeding farms that once were for the slave master's benefit in our own communities. Lots of children from different mothers but of the same father running around fatherless and being raised to be fed back into the very system that oppresses them. Of course, they have help whether unknowingly or knowingly as lots of things have been engineered to be so. Lack of knowledge, patience and understanding has been the downfall of many and what's kept the many harmful cycles going.

I hope from what I've written thus far women are able to recognize the power they hold in this earth. Especially, how the very words from their tongue can be used to speak life into a man (or anyone for that matter). I used Sacred as an example because I learned and matured the most while relating to her. I relearned myself and what it meant to be a man and even more so because she made it a safe space to do so.

It is women like Sacred that have inspired men to rule the world and make the impossible seem possible. When a woman believes in a man, she helps create a foundation in order for him to move towards his great feat with assuredness. Her wisdom can be the light that causes a man to shine in the darkness.

Women must realize this is just a portion of the potential they possess when they are operating at their optimal capacity and maturity. The power of a woman is actually beyond what's able to be measured.

"Sacred"

Thanks for your time and efforts!

MORE TO COME IN THIS POWER OF A WOMAN SERIES

THIS WORK IS BROUGHT TO YOU BY ROBERT GRAHAM
AND GRAHAMR WRITINGS LLC

Check out some of these other titles from authors on the GrahamR Writings roster on Amazon, Barnes & Noble & Google Play!

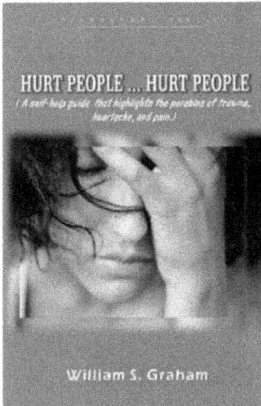

HURT PEOPLE ... HURT PEOPLE
(A self-help guide that highlights the paradox of trauma, heartache, and pain.)

William S. Graham

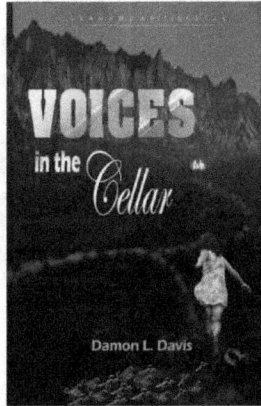

VOICES in the Cellar

Damon L. Davis

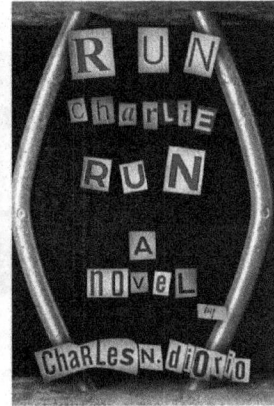

RUN charlie RUN

A novel by

ChaRLes N. diOrio

2Faces: The Saga

Ferguson

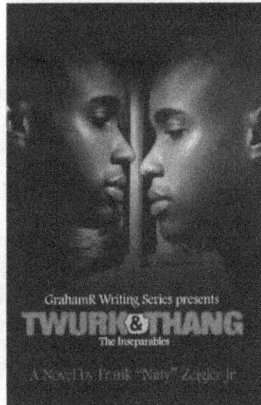

GrahamR Writing Series presents

TWURK & THANG
The Inseparables

A Novel by Frank "Naty" Zeigler Jr.

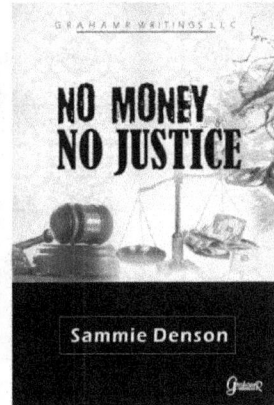

GRAHAMR WRITINGS LLC

NO MONEY NO JUSTICE

Sammie Denson

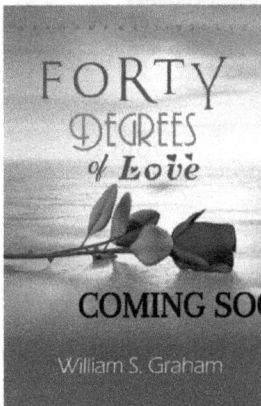

FORTY DEGREES of Love

COMING SOON IN JUNE!

William S. Graham

Presents

South Side

STOP

SOLO SEASON
BY SOLO SLIM

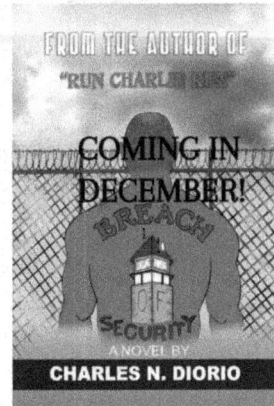

FROM THE AUTHOR OF "RUN CHARLIE RUN"

COMING IN DECEMBER!

BREACH

SECURITY

A NOVEL BY
CHARLES N. DIORIO

Also check out these titles on those same platforms!

We also have books written in Yoruba from our
international author from Nigeria!

(On Amazon)

You can find both of these titles on Barnes & Noble &
Google Books and Google Play!